To Gary:

Come back here bears
soon.

Love,
The Kindergarten

Feb. 1979

Scott

Gary

Allen

A Stepping-Stone Book

WATER FOR TODAY AND TOMORROW

BY
R. J. LEFKOWITZ

PICTURES BY LAWRENCE DI FIORI

Parents' Magazine Press • *New York*

for Margaret,
without whom not

Library of Congress Cataloging in Publication Data

Lefkowitz, R   J   1942-
  Water for today and tomorrow.

  (A Stepping-stone book)
  1. Water — Juvenile literature.   I. Di Fiori,
Lawrence, illus.   II. Title.
GB671.L38   553'.7   72-8094
ISBN 0-8193-0629-0 (lib. bdg.)

What's in This Book

Chapter 1
A Word about Water

Water is good stuff. There are so many things you can do with it!

Water is good for drinking, and for cooking things. You can take baths in it, and sail boats on it. Tropical fish and turtles can be kept in water, and dogs and cats can play in it.

And so can you. Water is great for swimming, splashing, and squirting at people—if they don't mind.

Besides all that, there's nothing like water for cleaning things. With water, we can get the dirt off cars and walls, dishes and balls, kittens and shelves, and even ourselves.

Water cleans your toes and washes your clothes. Also pots and pans and moving vans, not to mention toys and chairs and grizzly bears. Water cleans everything!

Well, *almost* everything. You can't clean a cookie with water, or an ice cream cone. The cookie will just crumble up, and the ice cream will melt away. If you poured a lot of water on them, they would seem to disappear. The water would *dissolve* them completely.

Water will clean most things, but a lot of things will get dissolved instead. And you don't always know which is going to happen!

Water is full of surprises like that.

7

Sometimes water surprises you just by being there when you hadn't noticed it.

That happens because water is often hard to see. It has no color at all, and you can look right through it. A bottle full of water looks almost the same as an empty one.

Have you ever stepped into a puddle or put your hand into water that you didn't know was there? Your nose can't warn you, the way it can about smoke or gasoline. Water has no smell at all.

Another thing that water doesn't have is taste. If that doesn't sound right to you, try to tell what water tastes like. Is it sweet or sour, bitter or salty? Can you think of *anything* that water tastes like—besides water?

Something else you might like to think about is what shape water has. That may be easy to tell when the water is in a bottle or a glass. But every time you pour the water into a new container, it gets a new shape. Water never has *any* shape of its own.

Do these things about water surprise you? No color, no smell, no taste, no shape—and no end of things you can use it for!

Chapter Two
Water All Around

Another odd thing about water is that once you start thinking about it, you start noticing it all around you.

Take a look around your home, and see how many places you can find water. It runs out of faucets in the kitchen and the bathroom. You may also be able to hear it running through pipes behind the walls or under the floors. There may be a faucet on the outside of your house, too.

Is that all the water in your home? Look harder, and you will find more. The trick is knowing it when you see it. Water can change the way it looks, and it can change its name, too.

If you look inside the freezer part of your refrigerator, you may find some ice cubes. Take one out and let it melt in the sink. Is there anything in the ice cube besides water? If you didn't think of ice cubes when you first started looking for water, it's probably just because, when water gets frozen, it changes from liquid to solid. And its name gets changed to *ice.*

You may be able to find more water in the refrigerator, under another name. The white, snowy-looking stuff that sometimes builds up in the freezer is called *frost*. But it's just another kind of frozen water. Put some frost in the sink to melt, and see for yourself.

When a kettle is put on the stove to boil,
water changes in another way. The hot water boils
right out of the kettle, and turns to *steam.*
Steam is very hot. If your home has radiators to
keep you warm in the winter, they probably
have steam in them.

Sometimes you can hear steam whistling in
a tea kettle or hissing in a radiator. But you can
never see steam at all. Still, there is something
you can see that will tell you when steam is around.

When steam cools down, it starts to *condense,* or change back to liquid water again. It forms tiny droplets. In the air, the water droplets can make a cloud.

Have you ever noticed a little cloud over a kettle or a radiator valve? The cloud tells you that there is steam just beneath it. The hot steam is condensing to water as it meets the cooler air above the kettle.

The air always has some water in it that you cannot see. The water is in such very tiny bits that most of the time you can't feel them, either. This water in the air is called water *vapor*.

Water vapor is very nearly the same thing as steam, but not so hot. You could think of steam as the special name for vapor that comes from boiling water. When it's cooler than that, it's just called vapor.

But just because water vapor is cooler than steam doesn't mean it isn't warm. Often it is very warm. When vapor cools, it condenses to form water in the same way that steam does. You might say that water vapor is something between ordinary water and steam.

Did you ever breathe against a windowpane indoors on a cold day? Water vapor in your breath gets cooled when it touches the cold glass. It condenses, and forms a *mist* on the windowpane.

Sometimes, when there is a lot of vapor in

the air, windows get so misted up that you can't even see through them. Then you may see water start to run down the windowpanes in tiny rivers.

When you go outside, you can find water almost everywhere. Perhaps you live near a big river, or even an ocean. Or maybe you live in the country, near a stream, a lake, or a pond.

Even if you live in a city, there is water
nearby. There may be ponds and fountains in the
parks, or in front of big buildings. And water
is always rushing beneath your feet, through pipes
and sewers.

There is water underground in the country, too. You may get water for your home from a well dug into the ground. Or you may know where there is an underground spring.

Even if you live in the desert, there is some
water beneath the ground. And there is more water
stored up in the plants that grow in the desert.
In the pioneer days, sometimes thirsty travelers got
water from cactus plants.

The more you look for water outside, the
more water you will find. Sometimes, when you
are least expecting it, water will fall right down
on your head! Then it's called rain!

On a very cold day, falling rain may freeze
into *sleet.* Or it may turn into the hard bits of ice
called *hail.*

There are still other names for water that
falls from the sky. Sometimes it's called snow.
Snow, like the frost in your freezer, is made
of water vapor that has frozen.

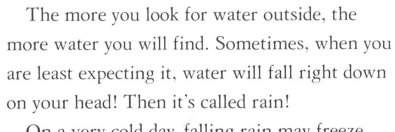

Mist can form outdoors when there is a lot of water vapor in the air. Then it feels very wet outside, almost as if it were raining.

A very heavy mist is called a *fog.* In a thick fog, you may hardly be able to see where you are going. You may feel as though you are walking in a cloud.

You are. The clouds high above your head are not very different from the fog that is near the ground. Like the clouds that form over tea kettles and radiators, the clouds in the sky are just big bunches of water droplets. When too much water builds up in the clouds, they let some of it go as rain or snow.

Some day in the summer, get up very early in the morning and find some grassy ground. The ground will probably feel very damp. You may think that it has rained during the night.

But it doesn't have to rain at night for the ground to be wet in the morning. Without the sun to keep it warm, the earth cools off during the

night. Water vapor in the air condenses on the cool ground. It makes the wetness you feel, called *dew.* But dew doesn't usually last very long. When the sun comes up, it quickly warms the earth and returns the dew to the air. The dew changes back to vapor again.

You won't find dew much in the winter. But then you may find frost on the ground, or on the outsides of windows. Can you figure out why?

In winter, you can also see icicles hanging from roofs and building ledges. Any time of year, you can find water almost everywhere you look.

Can you think of any big place where there is *no* water?

Chapter Three
Water Coming and Going

Water, water everywhere. Where does all the water come from? Where does it go?

Next time it rains or snows, think about how much water is falling from the sky. You could never count how many gallons of water are coming down.

That is where all of our water comes from. Do you wonder what would happen if the sky got all rained out?

That would not be a good thing. People could not live without water. No animal could live without water, and neither could any plant. If there were no more rain, nothing could live on the earth.

But the sky never does get all rained out.

When it rains, some of the water goes into the ground. But the earth can't soak up all of the water. Water runs along the ground in tiny rivers, called *rivulets.* After a snowfall, the melting snow makes rivulets, too.

Many rivulets running along the ground come together to make a brook. Then the brook bubbles along until it becomes part of a big stream. Water from many brooks may empty into the stream.

From all over, streams rush across the land toward a meeting-place. They end their journey at a mighty river. The river winds along, taking all the water to the ocean.

Many streams flow into the rivers, and many rivers go down to the sea. Nearly all of the water that runs along the earth finally finds its way to the ocean.

25

Some of the water that soaks into the ground
ends up in the ocean, too. But most of it goes along
underground to ponds and lakes. The ponds and
lakes store the water like tiny oceans. Nearly all of
the water that falls as rain ends up in ponds,
lakes, and oceans. Some of the rain falls right into
them.

When you look at a pond on a calm day, it
looks as if all the water is just sitting there. But it
isn't. Even though you can't see it happening,
some of the water is turning to vapor right before
your eyes. It is heat from the sun that makes the
water *evaporate.*

When the sun shines, water evaporates from ponds, lakes, puddles, and oceans. The water vapor rises high into the air, and makes clouds. Then the sky is ready to pour rain on us again.

Water is always going back and forth, up as vapor and down again as rain. That is why the sky never dries out. Even if it is not raining in one place, it may be raining some place else.

None of the water ever really gets used up. In time, all the water we use goes back up to the clouds, and then returns to earth for us to use again. The same water gets used over and over.

You may drink the same water that a dinosaur once drank!

Chapter Four
Water Comes to Town

People who live in the country are usually close
to the water they use. They may have wells in their
own back yards, or not very far away.

But in a city, there are no wells. Thousands
of people live in tall buildings that may have hardly
any water beneath them. Can you guess where
city people get the water to fill their sinks and tubs
and teacups?

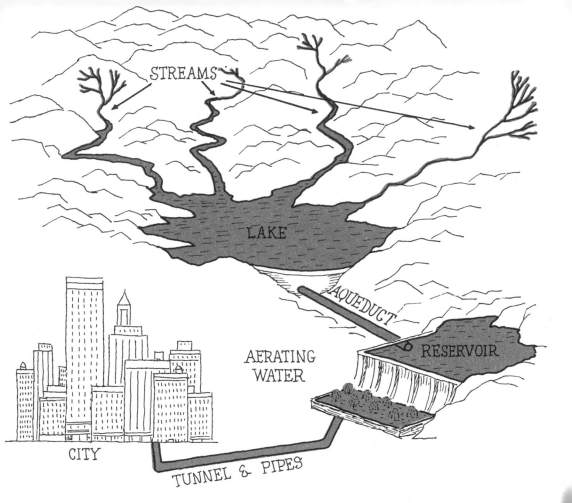

STREAMS

LAKE

AQUEDUCT

RESERVOIR

AERATING
WATER

CITY

TUNNEL & PIPES

Water for a city comes from a *reservoir*. A
reservoir is a kind of lake that the city uses
to collect and store its water. It may be a lake that
people have made themselves, or it may be one
that was already there. A reservoir can hold more
gallons of water than you could count between
now and your next birthday.

But it wouldn't take very long for all the people in their homes and offices and factories to use up the water in a reservoir. How does the reservoir keep on filling itself? Some rain falls on the reservoir, of course. But it would never be enough to keep the reservoir full.

Even though a reservoir usually isn't more than a few miles away from a city, the water for the reservoir may come from much farther away than that. It may come from hills and mountains hundreds of miles from the city. Rain and snow falling on the hills make streams, above ground and under it, that join together and run down to the reservoir.

The reservoir is made below the hills, so that gravity will help the water on its way. Gravity is what makes all things move downward on the earth.

Even though the reservoir is below the hills, it is usually above the city. That way, gravity can

help move the water down to where it is needed.
If the reservoir is below the city, or even on
the same level, then pumps are needed to push
the water along.

You never see the water coming to the city
from a reservoir, because it travels underneath the
ground. It moves through great pipes and tunnels—
so big you could stand up inside some of them.

31

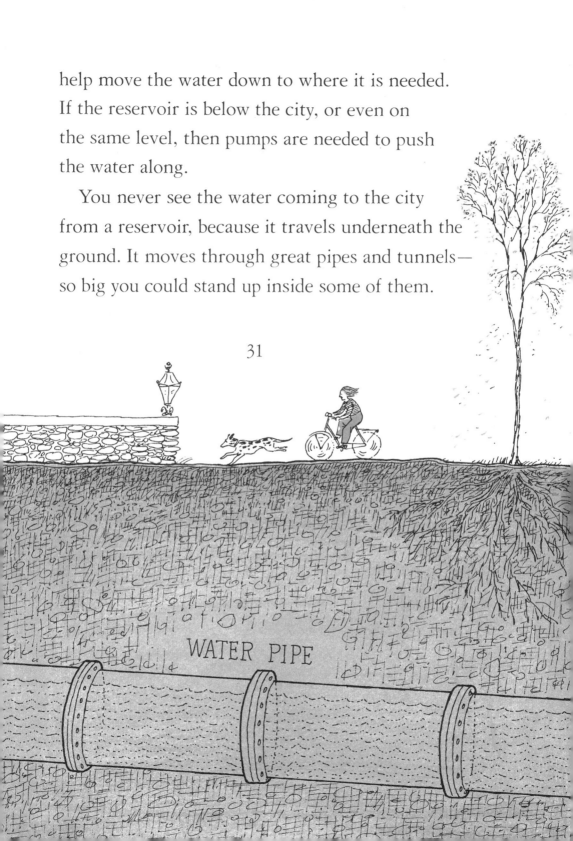

WATER PIPE

But water straight from the reservoir would not be good for drinking. It might contain dirt and germs and other things that could harm you. So the water has to be cleaned up before it gets to the city.

Some of the cleaning starts in the reservoir itself. While the water is standing around, waiting to be used, it is getting rid of some of the stuff that is washed into it by the streams. Heavy things, such as pebbles and clumps of soil, sink to the bottom of the still water. Gravity pulls them down.

But not everything sinks in the water. Some things float on top of the water, and some things swim in it. So before the water can get into the pipe that will take it to town, it has to go through a screen.

The screen is something like the ones you may use on your windows, only much bigger and heavier. It keeps out fishes, twigs, leaves, and all kinds of things. That is why you never have a frog popping into your bathtub.

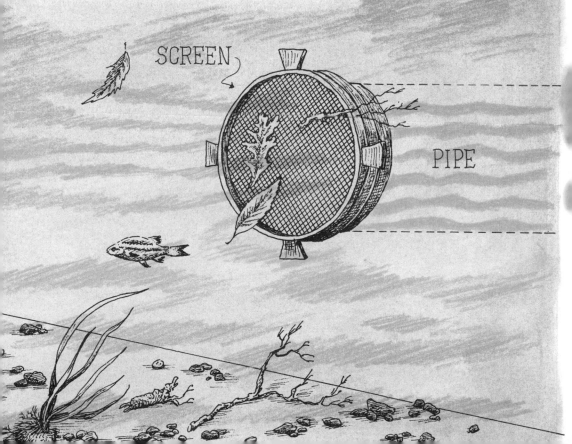

SCREEN

PIPE

Small things, such as little bits of soil, may still be in the water. They did not have enough time to settle to the bottom, and were small enough to go through the screen. So, many cities have special settling tanks for the water to go into after it leaves the reservoir.

In the settling tank, the water remains still for many days. Slowly the things in the water settle down to the bottom. Then the water is ready to move on again.

In many places the water may contain tiny bits of earth or rock that are too small and light even to sink down in the settling tank. Then the water will have to go through a filtering tank. The filtering tank is something like a strainer.

On the bottom of the tank is a layer of gravel, or small pieces of rock. On top of the gravel is sand. When water is let into the tank, it goes down through the sand and gravel, and out through small holes in the bottom of the tank. But the tiny

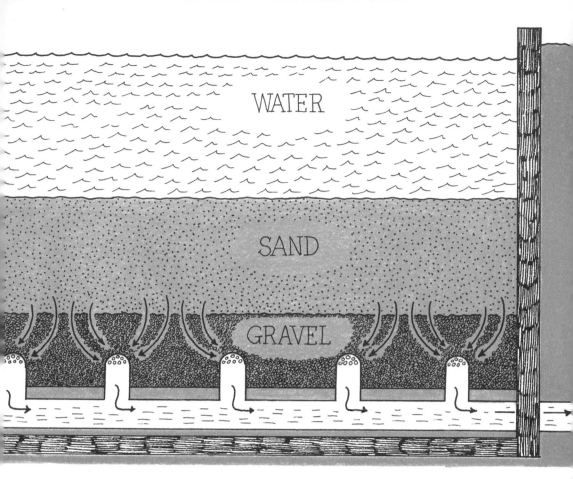

things that are in the water do not get to the
bottom of the tank. They get caught in the sand
and gravel. The sand and gravel are the filter in
the filtering tank.

Do you think the water is ready to drink
now? The people who take care of a city's water
supply wouldn't think so.

35

Even though the filtered water looks clear,
there can still be things in it we don't want. Germs
so tiny that they don't show in the water can
get through the screen and the filter, too. So most
cities add a chemical called chlorine to the
water, to kill the germs. (Some cities also add a
chemical called fluorine to the water, to help
keep our teeth from getting cavities.)

Other things that could be in the water are
gases. The gases might not harm you, but they

could make the water taste or smell bad. So the gases are removed by *aerating* the water—which just means airing it out.

Pumps shoot fountains of water high into the air. The gases go out of the water into the air, and some of the air goes into the water. After the water has been aerated, people usually say that it tastes fresher and smells better. What they really mean, of course, is that now it doesn't taste or smell at all.

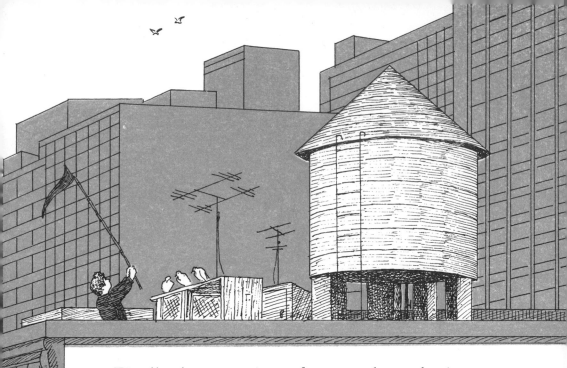

Finally the water is ready to go through pipes to the city. If the water came from high up in the hills, then it can travel up the pipes in an apartment building to get to the sinks on different floors. Water can always climb up until it is as high as the place where it came from.

In a very tall building, though, pumps might have to help the water get to the top. A tank on the roof can store the water. Then the water can flow down by gravity to the floors where it is needed.

After the water has been used for cooking or washing or some such thing, it becomes *waste water.* The waste water goes down through pipes that carry it off to the sewer.

In some places, the sewer may empty directly into a river or an ocean. But that is not a very good idea. The waste water is not clean, and enough of it can dirty up a whole river.

A better idea is to treat the water going out more or less the same way it was treated on the

way in. At the end of the sewer line, the water
is screened by screens, settled in settling tanks, and
filtered by filters. New germs that may have got
into the water are killed with chlorine. Now the
water can be safely let into a river, without
spoiling it.

Many cities today try to clean up their waste
water in this way, instead of just dumping it
carelessly into a river. They know that, sooner or
later, we will have to use that water again.

Chapter Five
What To Do with All the Water

If you look at a map of the world, you will see
that most of it is ocean. Water covers much more
of the earth than land does. And there is hardly
any land that does not have some water running
across it, or maybe sitting on it as a lake.

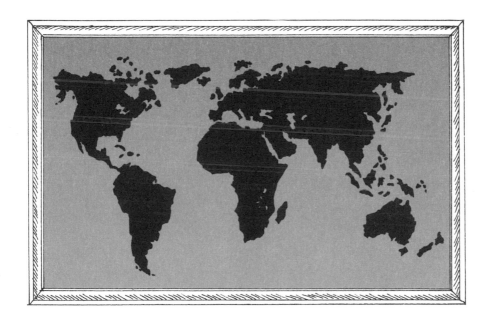

With all the water that's around, you might expect that people would think up lots of ways of using it. And they do.

Big ships and little sailboats travel on the oceans. Fishermen catch food in the water, and divers hunt for pearls and sponges. People swim in

the ocean for fun. Spacecraft splash down in it
for safety. They do that because the water is not so
hard as the ground.

Rivers do a lot more than just carry water
to the ocean. Boats can sail on big rivers, carrying
people and cargo from one town to the next.
  Sometimes factories are built along a river, so
that there will be a good supply of water. A lot
of water is needed for some of the things that go on
in factories.

Electric power plants are placed along
rivers, too. The running water can turn the
machines that make the electricity. Also,
the water can be used to keep the machines cool.

Power plants and factories both use the
river water to clean their floors and walls and
machines, and to flush away wastes. Nobody
likes a dirty power plant.

Water that stays in one place—like the water in a lake—can't turn any machines. But it can do other things besides letting people play in it.

If it is a very large lake, ships may be able to carry things across it. Smaller lakes are good for catching fish, or for growing them. And a factory can use the water in a lake if it has pumps to move the water around.

Everyone knows that rainwater helps plants
to grow. Without water, no plants could grow at all.
In places where there isn't enough rainfall,
farmers may pump water from a river to keep their
plants from dying.

Not just small plants like flowers and vegetables
need water, but the biggest trees, too. And so
do the animals that eat the plants and live among
the trees. Without water, the animals would
not just be thirsty. They would have nothing to eat
and no place to live. And neither would you.

In towns and cities, people use water to do things like making soup, mixing paints, and filling bird baths. Also peeling onions, flushing toilets, and getting labels off jars. People sit near fountains in the park because they like the way the splashing water looks and sounds and feels.

If you tried to make a list of all the things people do with water, you would probably wear out your pencil before you were finished. But without water, you would never have a pencil to begin with.

Can you figure out why?

48

Chapter Six
Water, for Better or Worse

The very first words in this book said that
water is good stuff. But sometimes you might think
that water is not so good at all. Ask anyone
whose bathtub has just overflowed, or whose picnic
has been ruined by the rain.

Water is the kind of thing that can seem good one moment, and bad the next.

Ships float on water, but sometimes they sink. People like to swim in water, but sometimes they drown. A river can help run a factory, but now and then it might flood the factory and the whole town.

A farmer needs water, but sometimes he gets more than he needs. Water running across the land can carry away soil that the farmer must have to grow his crops.

Trees need water to grow, but water can
make wooden things rot. Rain helps make iron
rust, and ruins shoes and party clothes. It gets
traffic all tied up, and makes it hard for airplanes to
take off and land.

Ice can make the ground slippery, and cause a lot
of accidents. A heavy snowfall makes it hard to
go anywhere. A lot of snow on a roof can sometimes
make the roof fall in.

Water does some terrible things!

Sometimes, whether water seems good or
bad depends on how much there is. If there's more
than we want, we don't like it. We might call it
a downpour, a flood, or a blizzard, and say it's a
nuisance.

Other times, different people may say the water
is good or bad, depending on how it affects
them. Children watching the snow fall might be

very happy, thinking about going sledding and building snowmen. But a man looking out the window might be thinking sadly about how he will have to shovel his walk and dig out his car.

Almost everything that water does can seem good to some people and bad to others. Often the same person might like or dislike water at different times, even when it is doing the same thing.

53

If a fire started in your home, you would be glad that water can put out fires. You might say that putting out fires is one of the best things water can do. But what do you think you would say if it rained while you were trying to build a campfire outdoors?

You might think it is surprising that water can seem so different to different people, or to the same people at different times. But most things in nature are like that.

Things like water, wind, and fire can seem like our best friends some of the time, and our worst enemies at other times. But they can't think about what they are doing, and they can never mean to be friendly or unfriendly.

Do you suppose we could ever really say that water is either "good" or "bad"? Mostly it seems to depend on whether we like what it's doing!

Chapter Seven
Watch Your Water!

Because there is so much water in the world, some people think we can do anything we like with it, and never have to worry about not having enough. But like many other things we would like to believe, that is not quite true.

For one thing, there is not as much water around as those people might think. At least, not water that we can *use.*

Much of the world's water is "tied up" as ice at the South and North Poles. If the ice caps at the

poles ever melted, the seas would rise. Many parts
of the earth would be flooded. But as long as
the ice caps are there, the water in them is locked
up tight.

People who live far up in the North can use the
ice and snow to build houses, if they need to.
But for most of us it is useless. We cannot drink it
or do anything else with it.

Oceans hold most of the world's liquid water. Oceans are good for sailing ships and catching fish, but they cannot give us water for drinking. The water in the sea has salt in it, and you would get sick if you drank very much of it. Nor can the salt water be used for washing or cooking.

In some places, people are building plants (like factories) that can get the salt out of sea water. Then the water can be used for many different things.

But most of us still depend on rain for our fresh water. Fresh water is water that does not have salt in it. Even though the rainwater might come from the ocean, it is fresh because the salt stays behind when the sea water evaporates into the air.

Has there ever been a water shortage in the town where you live? A water shortage happens when there is not enough rain to fill the reservoirs in a certain place. Then people have to be very careful of how much water they use.

Even when there isn't a shortage, it isn't very wise to waste water. Wasting it can make a shortage happen that much sooner. But often it takes a water shortage to make people think about using their water wisely.

Like the oceans, lakes and rivers also may contain water that we cannot use. Not that we would ever drink the water directly from a lake or river. But we might like to use it for swimming or boating. Yet sometimes we cannot use it even for that.

Water to go boating on doesn't have to be
quite as clean as drinking water. But it has to be
clean enough so that it doesn't look or smell
bad. If we want to go swimming in the water, then
it has to be at least clean enough not to get us
dirty.

A lake or a river hardly ever gets very dirty by
itself. But if a town or a factory pours a lot of
wastes into a lake, it can get dirty very quickly.
Then, even though the lake is still there,
nobody will be able to use it.

It doesn't even take a whole town or a big factory to mess up a lake. The people who enjoy the lake can do it all by themselves.

A lot of people might go rowing on the lake, and throw pop bottles and sandwich wrappers into it. Then the next year they might come back and say, "We don't like this lake any more! It's full of pop bottles and sandwich wrappers!"

Do you think that makes any sense?

All the water that was ever on the earth is still on the earth. And all the water that we have now, we will always have.

But, like anything else worth having, the water needs to be cared for. Because people have not cared for their water in the past, we do not have as much *usable* water as we once did. If people go on not caring for their water, we will have still less in the future.

That doesn't have to happen, though. If people just take a little time and trouble to treat their water carefully, then it will always be clean enough for everyone to use and have fun with.

Does *that* make any sense?

INDEX

63